The Creature Club

The Mountain Gorilla

By Melissa Kim

Illustrated by
Ann Strugnell

Ideals Children's Books • Nashville, Tennessee

Published by Ideals Publishing Corporation
Nashville, Tennessee 37214

Printed in Hong Kong.

ISBN 0-8249-8615-6 (pap)
ISBN 0-8249-8629-6 (lib)

Conceived, edited, designed, and produced by Signpost Books, Ltd.
Oxford, England OX3 0AB

Editor: Dorothy Wood
Designer: Gillian Riley

Library of Congress Card Catalog # 93-079972
Library of Congress Cataloging-in-Publication Data is available.

NOTICE TO QUIT

Please move out of your home at once. We do not know where you should go, but we know you will find somewhere. We do not know if you will find enough of the right sort of food to eat. And the climate may not be as warm as you are used to, but we need your space, so you must go.

The Management

Wouldn't it be terrible if this happened to you and your family? Yet every year, every week, every day, some kind of living creature disappears from the earth because it is forced to leave its natural home.

The mountain gorilla, for example, is in danger. It may seem a far away and remote creature, but you can help prevent the extinction of this magnificent animal.

If you care about animals in danger, you automatically become a member of The Creature Club. There is no membership fee, no clubhouse, no president—just people who share a common concern for animals and want to do something to make the world a better place for the mountain gorilla and for all of us.

Great ape family

CHIMPANZEES

Gorillas are the largest member of the great ape family, which includes chimpanzees and orangutans. The great apes belong to the animal order known as **primates,** which includes monkeys and humans. In fact, the great apes are our closest animal relatives. Primates are mammals—warm-blooded animals that produce milk to feed their young. The babies of gorillas, chimpanzees, and orangutans spend several years with their parents.

GORILLAS

FACT FILE

Gorillas have no natural enemies apart from people.

ORANGUTANS

The gorilla file

Not all gorillas are alike. Gorillas fall into three main categories, according to their size, their habits, and where they live. Eastern and western lowland gorillas live on plains and at the base of mountains. Mountain gorillas live high up in the mountains, sometimes as high as 11,500 feet (3,500 meters).

A

B

C

FACT FILE

Who's who here?
Look at the descriptions and try to identify the different gorillas.
Then look for the answers on page 32.

Mountain gorillas have been endangered for many years. Learning about them and why they are endangered is like putting together a puzzle. To find all the pieces you need to ask a series of questions.

Name: Western Lowland Gorilla	
Address:	**Important features:**
Africa	Short black hair
Lives mainly in Cameroon,	Wide skull
Central African Republic,	Long arms and legs
Gabon, and the Congo.	Thin hands
	Wide hips
Population: Estimated at 39,000	

Name: Eastern Lowland Gorilla	
Address:	**Important features:**
Africa	Fairly short dark hair
Lives mainly in Zaire	Narrow skull
and Uganda.	Long arms
	Thin hands
	Wide hips
Population: ENDANGERED Estimated between 3,000 and 5,000	

Name: Mountain Gorilla	
Address:	**Important features:**
Africa	Long, thick black hair
Lives mainly in mountains	Broad, long jaw
of Virunga Volcanoes area	Short arms and legs
where Uganda, Rwanda,	Long torso
and Zaire intersect.	Short, broad hands
Some also live in Bwindi	Thin hips
Forest in Uganda.	
Population: ENDANGERED Estimated at 600	

Where can mountain gorillas be found?

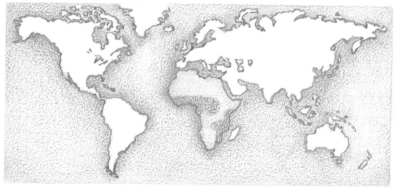

A mountain gorilla is a rare sight. This elusive animal can be found only in one small corner of the world.

Look carefully at this map of Africa.

- Can you find Zaire (ZAH-eer), Uganda, and Rwanda (ru-WAN-da)?

- Place a sheet of tracing paper over the map and color in these three countries.

- Make a circle around the spot where the three countries meet.
  These are the Virunga Mountains where mountain gorillas live.

8

How many are there?

Hundreds of years ago, **mountain gorillas** roamed parts of central Africa. By the 1950s there were only about 500 of them left. In 1982 scientists counted about 255 in the Virunga Volcanoes area and about 120 in the Bwindi forest. Since then the mountain gorilla population has slowly risen, but there are still only about 600 in existence.

The number of **lowland gorillas** is harder to determine. Many lowland gorillas live in forests too isolated for humans to easily explore. However, scientists feel certain that there are more lowland than mountain gorillas.

Some gorillas live in zoos. Most of these are **western lowland gorillas**. Only about 1Q to 15 **eastern lowland gorillas** live in zoos.

Counting gorillas is not easy in the wild. Scientists use several different methods to track, identify, and count the different gorilla groups.

Some scientists have actually lived with gorillas. They get to know each gorilla individually. This is the best way to keep track of a population, but it's difficult to do for every group of gorillas, because some live in places where humans would find it difficult to survive.

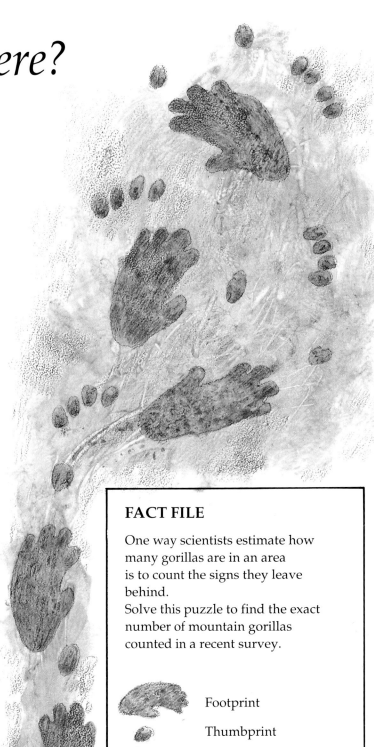

FACT FILE

One way scientists estimate how many gorillas are in an area is to count the signs they leave behind.
Solve this puzzle to find the exact number of mountain gorillas counted in a recent survey.

Footprint

Thumbprint

Knuckle print

Count the prints:

Footprints   _ _ _ _   x 100
Thumbprints   _ _ _ _ _   x 10
Knuckle prints   _ _ _ _   x 1

Total number of
mountain gorillas

(Answer on page 32.)

Let's count the gorillas in this picture.

Minimum number = the number of gorillas you can actually see.

Maximum number = the number of signs the gorillas have left behind plus the number of gorillas you can see.

GORILLA SIGNS

Nests

Droppings

Flattened Plants

Food remains

Knuckle prints

How many gorillas do you see?
How many signs can you find?
(Answers on page 32.)

What are mountain gorillas like?

If you have a picture in your mind of gorillas ripping up trees, casting aside small animals, and beating their chests, put it aside. Gorillas are actually very peaceable animals, and not at all dangerous. They rarely fight with each other, and they certainly don't fight with other species.

FACT FILE

Beating the chest is part of a "display." There are nine parts to a display. Only the **silverbacks**, the male gorillas who act as leaders of a group, perform all nine parts. Others may perform only a few of the parts.

- Hoot
- Pretend to eat
- Rise on two legs
- Throw plants
- Beat chest
- Kick legs
- Run around
- Hit or tear out plants
- Thump on the ground

Gorillas usually make a display when they're afraid or when they think one of the group is in danger. The display involves mainly noise and arm-waving and is meant to scare off the person or animal of whom the gorilla is afraid.

All mountain gorillas live in groups. These groups, which are like large families, are very important to the gorilla's way of life. Although males may spend many years alone, it is difficult for a gorilla to live without a group forever.

Gorilla groups often include females from several different families, so not all the members are actually related by blood. While the average group has eight to ten members, a group with nearly 30 members has been recorded.

Each group has a leader who protects the group members. He decides when and where to travel, rest, eat, and sleep.

As male gorillas get older, the hair on their backs turns from black to gray, or silver. The leader is one of these older males, called a silverback. Usually there is one silverback in each group.

The group also includes black-backed males, females with babies, single females, and young gorillas. The babies cling to their mothers' bellies; when they are a little older, they ride on their mothers' backs.

Make your own personal and family information sheet and fill it in.

Adult males, aged 10 to 14 years, weigh about 330 pounds (150 kg), twice as much as the average female. The average male is about 5 ft. 8 in. tall (1.7 m).

A day in the life of a gorilla

6:30 - 7:30 A.M.: Wake up (about a half hour after sunrise).

7:30 - 10:45 A.M.: Spend a few hours eating.

10:45 - 11 A.M.: Pick a spot, beat down the plants, and clear out a nice area in which to rest.

11 A.M. - 2 P.M.: Rest period. Young gorillas may play, others groom themselves, and others sleep.

2 - 4 P.M.: Time for more eating.

4 - 5 P.M.: Travel time. If the group has to move to a new site, this is the best time of day to travel.

5 - 7 P.M.: Once the leader has chosen a place to spend the night, it's nest-building time. All nests need to be finished by sunset.

Gorillas don't wander aimlessly from place to place. They live in an area called a **home range.** Each group stays in one large area of about 4 square miles (10 sq. km). The home ranges of different groups can overlap, but gorillas are happy to let other animals share their home range. They don't defend their territory the way a dog might. They just live in it. They travel quite a bit within the home range, mostly in search of food.

FACT FILE

Mountain gorillas make a new nest every night. It only takes a few minutes to do so, and here's how:

1. Start as soon as the leader starts to make his nest. It's usually about an hour before sundown.

2. Break off any branches, herbs, or other plants that look suitable.

3. Use the plants to make a circle or half-circle around the body. The bottom of the nest is not important— it's the outside rim that really matters.

4. Then settle in! Sleep either on the side, with arms and legs tucked in, or on the stomach.

What do gorillas eat?

Mountain gorillas are very choosy eaters, so it may take a while to find just the right kinds of food. They're very picky about the part of the plant they eat. Besides their favorite foods (below), they also eat stems and roots, and some berries and other fruit. They don't eat meat but occasionally dig open an ants' nest to eat the eggs.

Gorillas rarely drink. Most of the liquid they take in comes from the food itself. Each gorilla searches for its own food, except for the young who must get help from adults.

AMBOBO OTHOSS

FACT FILE

Here are the mountain gorilla's five favorite foods. You can find out what they are by unscrambling the captions. Do the pictures give you any clues? (Answers on page 32.)

WDIL LRYECE   TSELTHI

TENLETS

KARB

Where do gorillas live?

The area where an animal lives and eats is its **habitat**. Gorillas can survive only in places where the specific plants they feed on are growing. And there needs to be enough food for the whole group.

The mountain gorilla's habitat is the tropical forest, also called the jungle—although jungle is not a scientific term. A **tropical forest** is often defined by its temperature and rainfall. Any place that is hot enough and wet enough can be called a tropical rainforest. In some rainforest areas, it rains and is as hot as 80° all year round!

Rainforests are full of epiphytes, or plants that grow on other trees, branches, and leaves. An orchid is a common epiphyte (EP-uh-fite).

Rainforests also contain lianas (lee-AH-nuhs). These are climbing plants, such as vines. They can be hundreds of yards long!

What is in a tropical forest?

There are many types of tropical forests. Mountain gorillas used to live mainly in mountain forests but now can be found even in the alpine forests, about 1,200 yards higher.

High in the mountains of the central African tropical forests, between 4,265 and 11,485 feet (1,300 to 3,500 m) above sea level, there are both rainy and dry seasons. The weather is cool and often very misty. The average temperature is 48 to 54°F, and there are often hail and frost. On the average, about 80 inches (200 cm) of rain falls each year in these areas.

18

Alpine forest

At the top of the mountains, about 11,500 feet (3,500 m) and more above sea level, the land becomes an alpine forest which looks more like a barren moonscape than a jungle. Mountain gorillas can be found even here!

Hagenia and Hypericum forest

Between 8,500 and 11,500 feet (2,600 to 3,500 m) above sea level, the forest is named after two dominant plants, *hagenia* and *hypericum*. The hagenia forest is like the mountain forest, but it is less dense, with smaller shrubs and herbs.

Bamboo forest

Higher up than the canopy, at about 8,200 feet (2,500 m), bamboo forests grow. The young bamboo shoots pop up during the heaviest rainy seasons, usually from October to December. Their canopy is lower than that of the evergreens, about 13 to 20 feet (4 to 6 m) high.

Mountain forest

At the bottom of these mountain forests is a layer of vegetation made up of plants and shrubs. There are herbs, ferns, mosses, and hundreds of other plants all densely packed together.

Next come the broadleaf evergreen trees, which are green all year round. Broadleaf trees have leaves rather than needles like those on pine trees.

The tops of trees grow together and form a canopy, usually about 50 feet (15 m) high. It's like a roof made of tree branches and leaves. If the canopy is really thick, not much sunlight or water reaches the bottom layer, and only hardy shrubs will survive.

What is happening to the tropical forest?

The loss of forest areas is a major threat to the mountain gorilla's survival. People have cut down much of these areas and have a variety of reasons for doing so. Rwanda, for example, is the most heavily populated country in Africa, so its people cleared the forest to make room for themselves and to grow food and raise cattle. The bamboo and trees can also be burned as fuel and for building materials. Many people in these areas are poor and need to make money, so they have cleared the forest for timber and to grow crops to sell. Part of Rwanda's tropical forest was cleared to grow pyrethrum (pie-REE-thrum), a plant that is used to make insecticides that are sold worldwide.

The people of Rwanda are now conserving the forest. They have realized that while clearing the forest may bring in money today, it will cost dearly tomorrow. The forest is a vital part of the environment. It helps prevent floods, mud slides, and drought. And it is home to thousands of plants and animals.

FACT FILE
East Africa Facts at a Glance

RWANDA
Area: 10,166 sq. miles (26,338 sq. km)
Population: 7,276,000
Average Density: 716 people per sq. mile (276 per sq. km)
Capital: Kigali
Main industries: Agriculture, livestock
Exports: Coffee, tea, sugar, pyrethrum, tin bark of quinine

ZAIRE
Area: 905,328 sq. mi. (2,345,409 sq. km)
Population: 33,991,000
Average density: 38 people per sq. mi. (14 per sq. km)
Capital: Kinshasa
Main industry: Palm oil production
Exports: Coffee, rubber, cocoa, timber, copper, crude oil

UGANDA
Area: 91,110 sq. mi. (236,036 sq. km)
Population: 16,811,000
Average density: 185 people per sq. mi. (71 per sq. km)
Capital: Kampala
Main export: Coffee

The average density in the US is 68 people per sq. mile (26 per sq. km).

The average density in the UK is 601 people per sq. mile (232 per sq. km).

In a typical mountain forest, the canopy acts as an umbrella and prevents the soil from getting drenched.

Some of the water held in the canopy and roots evaporates and turns into rain again. In areas where the forest has been cleared, there has been a lot less rain. In the long term, less rain means droughts.

The roots soak up water and let it seep out slowly. They also hold the soil together to prevent mudslides and keep the rivers from flooding during the rainy season.

Can the gorillas survive these changes?

As the tropical forest is cleared, the gorillas have fewer places to live and less food to eat. Many problems arise from these difficult conditions.

- If more groups are forced to live in a smaller area, they'll be forced to compete for food. This would affect their naturally peaceful way of life.

- Gorillas can't cross rivers or lakes because they can't swim. This prevents them from travelling long distances to find new homes.

- Every year gorillas die from diseases associated with humans, such as malaria, pneumonia, and hookworm. Infant gorillas are usually hardest hit. Illnesses could increase with the strain of adapting to a new home.

- As mountain gorillas are forced higher and higher into the mountains, the colder climate adds to the number of illnesses that already afflict them. More and more of them catch pneumonia.

- Mountain gorillas aren't tree-climbers. If a gorilla is forced to climb a tree, it can fall out and hurt itself.

What else harms the gorillas?

The only creatures gorillas have to fear are humans.

● Humans began hunting gorillas more than 100 years ago. Gorillas' skins were sold to collectors or displayed to show the hunter's bravery.

● Hunting for sport is less popular now.

But poachers still trap gorillas and sell their skulls and hands, which are made into souvenir ashtrays.

● Poachers also hunt other animals in the forest. Gorillas can stumble into their traps and lose hands or feet. Some are forced into hiding, often into areas where they can't find food.

FACT FILE

Here are six different animals and six groups of products that are made from parts of their bodies. Match the product to the animal. The answers are on page 32.

Do you think these products are necessary? Can you think of substitutes for them?

What's being done to help mountain gorillas?

The future of the mountain gorilla is looking brighter, due to the work of private organizations and the governments of the African nations. However, the mountains where most of the gorillas live are spread across three separate countries, each of which has its own policy toward gorillas.

RWANDA

In 1979 animal scientists and concerned people from around the world joined together to form the Mountain Gorilla Project. This group works with Rwandans to study and protect mountain gorillas. The members travel around schools and villages, meeting people and showing films. They discuss gorillas, what can be done to help them, and how important it is to preserve their habitat.

The area of Rwanda where gorillas live is called the Parc National des Volcans, or Volcanoes National Park. It is a gorilla reserve, and poaching is forbidden. It is claimed that there has been no poaching in this part of the park since 1983, but the laws are hard to enforce.

ZAIRE AND UGANDA

Both Zaire and Uganda have formed groups similar to the Mountain Gorilla Project. The 300 mountain gorillas who live in Uganda's Bwindi Forest National Park seem fairly safe. The forest is so dense and thick that it's difficult for any people to live or work there, including poachers.

In the areas of the Parc National des Volcans that belong to Uganda and Zaire, there is less poaching now than in the past. But some poachers still capture babies and sell them to zoos, and adult gorillas are sometimes hurt or killed trying to defend their young.

Why would a zoo buy from poachers? Sometimes someone will bring to the zoo a baby that's already been captured, so the zoo takes it in to keep it alive. Some people claim that the best way to help gorillas survive is to breed them in zoos. They reason that if gorillas in the wild die out, there will be enough gorillas in zoos to start a new population. Most gorilla scientists disagree with this theory.

FACT FILE

Goals of the gorilla projects:

• Continue to work against poaching.

• Keep a close watch over the gorilla population.

• Educate people about the need to protect gorillas.

• Encourage tourists to visit the gorillas in order to raise money to help them.

What's it like on a gorilla watch?

Imagine sitting within touching distance of real, live mountain gorillas, breathing in their scent, and watching their babies at play.

Each year, more and more people visit Rwanda and Zaire to do just that. A guide takes small groups of people up into the mountains where several groups of gorillas will now let people come close to them.

These trips have become so popular that tourism is now one of Rwanda's three largest industries!

FACT FILE

NOTES

Clothes list:

Long pants
Hiking boots
Long-sleeved shirt
Rain jacket
Lightweight gloves

They told us not to bring anything that could get tangled in branches. And although it will be hot, we'll need to protect our arms and legs from the trees and bushes. A pullover will help since it feels chilly when you stop hiking.

DAY ONE

Flew to Kigali, the capital of Rwanda, then spent half a day driving through the cleared jungle to get to the park headquarters at Kinigi. There are six of us in my group and six in another group. There are no young children. I think the guides were concerned that children might be scared, or might scare the gorillas!

DAY TWO

Started our hike up the mountain. It took several hours, and was very hard work, because it was wet and we climbed to about 8,000 feet (2,500 meters).

At the park edge, we were trained in what to do when faced with an angry gorilla. If you feel afraid, or if the gorilla seems angry or aggressive, you should kneel and keep your head down. You should always move slowly. This makes the gorilla feel superior. Also, never get between two gorillas, especially a mother and her baby!

DAY THREE

Some other tips: No flash photography. Don't touch the gorillas or let them touch you. Don't point at a gorilla and don't leave any litter!

We hiked to where the gorilla group had last been sighted. The guide told us to keep low and stay behind him. We tracked the group to find the nests where they had spent the night. We finally found the gorillas after about two hours of walking from there.

There were ten gorillas in the group. They didn't seem surprised or afraid of us. They looked at us but didn't really move. The silverback looked huge, as if he would be bigger and much heavier than a tall man standing upright.

We watched them eat and sleep. The young ones played and wrestled with each other. One gorilla came up to smell me. He got so close that I could see the hairs on his chest. We looked at each other with curiosity and, I think, friendship. It wasn't until he walked away that I realized I had been holding my breath!

Why save mountain gorillas?

Here are some good reasons for making sure the mountain gorilla survives:

• Destroying the tropical forest is bad for everybody in the long run. Our environment is made up of many parts that all depend on each other. If some of those parts are taken away, the system doesn't work.

• As many kinds of birds and animals as possible must be allowed to survive. Saving the rainforest for gorillas means saving it for many other kinds of birds and animals.

• Humans can learn a lot about themselves by studying gorillas and the other great apes. They are our closest relatives in the animal kingdom.

• Some people believe that no animal, including man, should do things that harm another living thing unless there is absolutely no alternative.

What can we do to help?

• Write the governments of Rwanda, Zaire, and Uganda, telling them what you've learned and asking them to help the gorillas as much as they can.

• Write to the animal groups that work to protect gorillas, and give them your support.

• Try fundraising with your friends. Ask if you can set up collection boxes in a local library or shops to raise money to help the animal groups. Organize a sponsored gorilla walk.

• Write to your nearest zoo. Many have "Adopt-an-Animal" programs, in which you can donate money to feed an animal of your choice. (Warning! It costs a lot to feed a big gorilla for a year.) You'll probably get a photo of your animal and regular zoo news.

• Volunteer to collect for the World Wide Fund for Nature flag day.

• Anything you do to help is worthwhile. And remember, once you help support or protect an endangered animal, you become an honorary member of **The Creature Club**. Welcome to the Club!

FACT FILE

Here are the addresses of some of the groups that help gorillas:

African Wildlife Foundation
1717 Massachusetts Avenue, N.W.
Washington, D.C. 20036

World Wildlife Fund, Inc.
1250 24th Street, N.W.
Washington, D.C. 20037

The Digit Fund
P.O. Box 25
Ithaca, New York 14851

Why don't you write to one of these groups? They can give you more information about mountain gorillas and how you can help them.

The Gorilla Game

for 2 or more players, game pieces, & dice.

Throw 6 to start

Start here

1

2

3

4

5

Meet a scientist, move to 6 (11)

7

Can't find food, 8 go back to (1)

9

10

11

26

27

28

29

30 Poachers! Go back to (4)

31 Safe from poachers, go to (38)

32

33 Baby falls from tree, miss a turn

34

35

36 Build safe night-nest

37

38

39 Youngster caught in trap, miss a turn

46

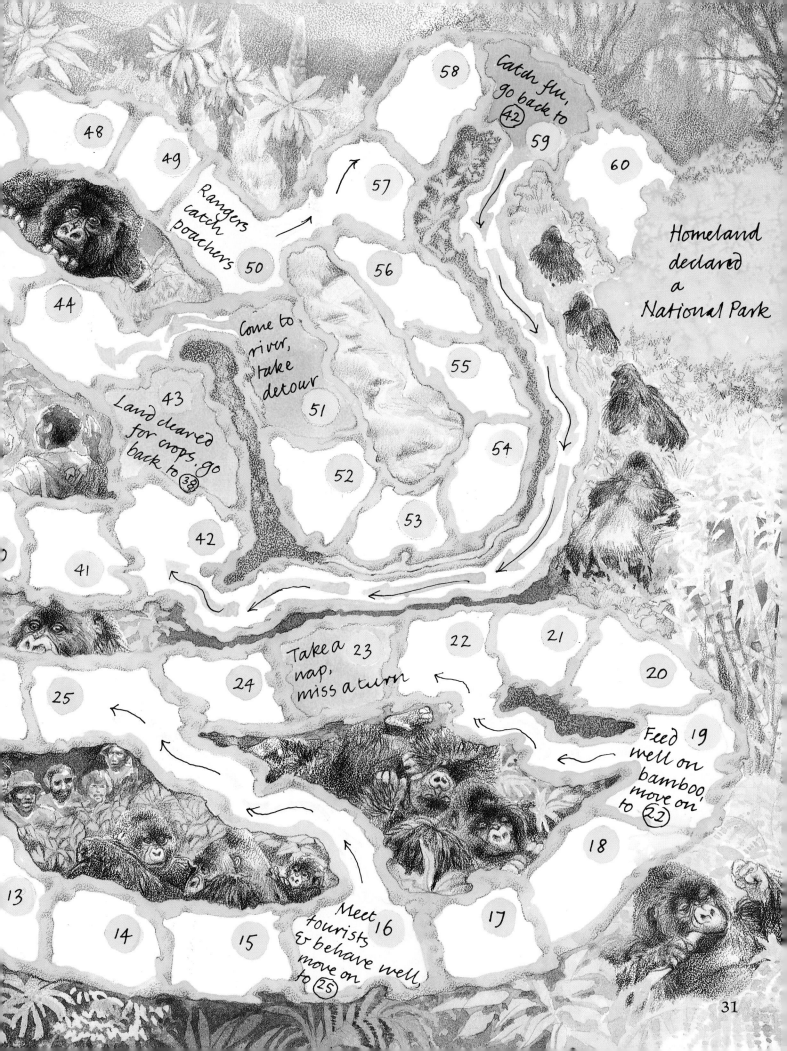

48

49

Rangers catch poachers

50

57

58

Catch flu, go back to 42

59

60

Homeland declared a National Park

56

44

Come to river, take detour

43

51

Land cleared for crops, go back to 38

55

52

54

42

53

41

23

Take a nap, miss a turn

22

21

24

20

25

Feed well on bamboo, move on to 22

19

18

13

Meet tourists & behave well, move on to 25

16

17

14

15

Index

Answers

Page 6-7:
A is the eastern lowland gorilla.
B is the mountain gorilla.
C is the western lowland gorilla.

Page 9:
5 footprints = 500
9 thumbprints = 90
4 knuckle prints = 4
Total: 594

Page 10-11:
Minimum number = 4
Maximum number = 8

Page 15:
Bamboo shoots; wild celery; thistle; nettles; bark

page 22-23:
Gorillas—hand and skull ashtrays
Crocodiles—handbags and shoes
Black rhino and elephants—ivory carvings and
  dagger handles
Sea turtles—bracelets and combs
Spotted cats—fur coats

Alternatives
Hand and skull ashtrays—plastic, glass
Handbags and shoes—canvas, vinyl, rubber, nylon
Ivory dagger handles, carvings $\}$ plastic, wood
Bracelets, combs
Fur coats—fur-like fabric